LITTLE BOOK OF

TV CARS

LITTLE BOOK OF
TV CARS

First published in the UK in 2014

© Demand Media Limited 2014

www.demand-media.co.uk

Printed and bound in Europe

ISBN 978-1-910270-09-7

Contents

Introduction

For as long as there has been cinema and television, cars of all shapes and sizes have been drafted in to supplement the action or drive the plot. From the earliest silent movies, where cars were routinely raced and destroyed, to the iconic cars on the small and big screen, this little book looks at the best-known cars in the history of entertainment. We'll uncover the stories behind the cars as well as featuring some of the most popular cars of all time, from Herbie and the General Lee to James Bond's Aston Martins and Lotus Esprit. Steve McQueen's 1968 Ford Mustang GT Fastback from the film *Bullitt* stars alongside the A-Team's van, Michael Knight's unforgettable talking car, KITT, and Batman's various Batmobiles. No book on screen cars would be complete without the Trotters' Reliant Regal, Lady Penelope's Rolls-Royce, Mr Bean's Mini, the Ford Gran Torino from Starsky & Hutch, Magnum's red

Ferrari 308 and the 1959 Cadillac from *Ghostbusters*. This lavishly illustrated book examines the role of the car on screen and tells the story of the best-loved and most famous cars in the world.

The Ford Gran Torino from Starsky & Hutch

Starsky & Hutch became one of the most popular cop shows of the 1970s. Created by William and Ryan Blinn, and starring David Soul as Ken 'Hutch' Hutchinson and Paul Michael Glaser as David Starsky, the series combined police procedural with buddy cop drama. The enduring image from the series had nothing to do with its stars, however. The red and white Ford Gran Torino became one of the most famous screen cars in history after it debuted in the pilot.

When producer Aaron Spelling first showed Glaser the car, the actor was distinctly underwhelmed, claiming it was big, ugly and childish, and that it would never be used by undercover cops. David Soul was equally disparaging, saying it looked like a striped tomato. The nickname stuck and was eventually

worked into the script whenever Hutch wanted to wind up his partner. (Glaser had to ask the producers to modify the interior with bucket seats because every time he took a right-hand turn, Soul would fly across the cabin into him.)

Despite its size and apparent power and speed, the stock 1975 Windsor 351-powered (5.8-litre) V8 Gran Torino was an unwieldy and lacklustre brute to drive, and the enormous engine only managed to put out 202 horsepower. High-performance engine notes had to be dubbed over the original rumbling, while modifications had to be made to the chassis and suspension to get the car to behave during the stunt sequences. Even the gear ratios had to be adjusted to give the near-two-ton car better acceleration.

After the success of the pilot, two cars were used for the majority of filming in

Above: *A replica of the 1974 Ford Gran Torino driven by Starsky & Hutch*

the first season. They were fitted with modified 400-cubic-inch (6.6-litre) V8s for extra grunt, while the paintwork was also upgraded. For the second season, another two cars were ordered (they can be distinguished by the silver bumper filler panels, luxury chrome mirrors and body side mouldings. Power was upped again (from 224 to 280hp) as the engines had been enlarged to 460 cubic inches (7.5 litres).

The stunt driving sequences resulted in a large number of crashes but, as the show was broadcast weekly, the damage had to be repaired quickly. Some of the repairs were extremely sloppy and dents, scratches and scuffs to the paintwork are visible in many subsequent shots. Parts of trim and the licence plates are also often missing. Such was the success of the series, however, that Ford released a special-edition Torino in 1976. One was immediately procured by the producers as backup for the cars that were used in the final series. When shooting finished, the cars were bought by collectors, some of whom restored them to their original factory condition while others left the damaged panels in place to ensure authenticity.

LITTLE BOOK OF **TV CARS**   7

Batman's Batmobiles

The original Batmobile appeared in the DC Comics in the late 1930s, although it was then a red convertible sedan and didn't acquire the tailfins or gadgets until later. By 1941 the car had evolved into a high-powered streamlined vehicle that had a large single fin at the back and a bat's head motif on the front.

When Batman graduated to the small screen in 1966, the comics adopted his outrageous Batmobile with its twin rear fins, black colour scheme and complex gadgetry. The TV show wasn't popular with fans of the comics because of its camp humour and ridiculous plots but the car became an instant hit.

Bringing it to the screen had been particularly difficult, however. A year before the show was due to air, 20th Century Fox contacted veteran vehicle modifier Dean Jeffries and asked him to build a car for Batman and Robin. He began with a 1959 Cadillac but the network then brought the shooting schedule forward and he had to pull out. George Barris took on the project instead, and, when he too realised that time wouldn't allow him to build a car from scratch, he chose to modify a 1955 Lincoln Futura Concept Car, which had been created by Ford's in-house design team of Bill Schmidt, Doug Poole and John Najjar, as well as Lincoln's own styling department.

In just three weeks, Barris and metalworker Bill Cushenbery had built the Batmobile for the pilot at a cost of only $30,000. For the first season, they repainted it gloss black and added gadgets like a cable cutter, projector, Batphone, parachutes, smoke screen and battering ram, amongst many others. The two-ton car may have looked incredible but the original engine wasn't up to the job so it was replaced with a 390-cubic-inch (6.4-litre) Ford FE V8. The series only ran for three seasons and 120 episodes, after which falling ratings forced ABC executives to pull the plug. NBC offered to produce another series but the set had already been dismantled and they had no interest in paying another million to rebuild it.

Such was the popularity of the show that toymakers Mattel made a fortune with their scale versions of the Batboat and the Batmobile (which was produced under licence in the UK by both Matchbox and Corgi). Warner Brother acquired the merchandising rights in 2012, which allowed them to cash in on the updated versions of the car driven by Christian Bale's caped crusader. The original full-size Barris car sold at auction for $4.6 million to Richard Champagne in 2013. Several fibreglass copies and replicas that were built by the same team for promotional purposes are also in private collections.

The Batmobile returned to the big screen in Tim Burton's gothic masterpiece in 1989. This car was designed by Anton Furst and based on the chassis of a Chevy Impala. It was laden with gadgets such as bombs, machineguns and grappling hooks, as well as being powered by a gas turbine

engine. In this specification, the car (all 22 feet of it) could hit 60mph in 3.7 seconds and accelerate on to 330mph.

Although this incarnation was adapted for later films in the franchise, Christopher Nolan's 2005 revamp introduced a completely different Batmobile that was half Lamborghini and half tank. Six were built for various stages of filming, while a 1/3 scale electric model performed most of the stunts. It was equipped with dual cannons, a rocket launcher, landing hook, jet engine, armour plating and a 500-horsepower 5.7-litre GM V8 capable of propelling the 2.5-ton car to 60mph in 5.6 seconds.

Above: *The original screen Batmobile bore little resemblance to the car from the comics*

KITT from Knight Rider

The original KITT (Knight Industries Two Thousand) appeared in the TV series *Knight Rider* that ran from 1982 until 1986. The show's premise was that billionaire Wilton Knight rescued Detective Michael Long after he was shot in the face. His organisation (the Foundation for Law and Government) then recruited Michael (under a new identity – Michael Knight) as a field agent to fight crime. David Hasselhoff was chosen to play the part of Michael in one of the iconic action series of the 1980s.

Wilton Knight's organisation was run on a day-to-day basis by Devon Miles (Edward Mulhare), and he was assisted by technician Bonnie Barstow (Patricia McPherson). They operated out of a huge mobile command centre/garage that was a converted GMC General truck. Michael needed a car of course, so Devon provided him with a 1982 Pontiac Firebird Trans Am that had been modified with a host of special features.

Turbo boost gave rapid acceleration to 200mph or for jumping obstacles; the car could drive itself; its reaction time was a nanosecond and it had storage capacity of 1,000 megabits; it also boasted electromagnetic hyper-vacuum disc brakes that could slow it from 70mph to zero in just 14 feet (4.25 metres); and it had a flame thrower, tear-gas launcher and microwave jammer.

KITT's armour was a molecular bonded shell that could withstand the impact from almost any projectile or explosive, while its central processing unit was so advanced that it could learn to interact with humans and even developed an ego. KITT's CPU also contained an enormous variety of scanners and sensors that allowed it to track movement around the car when in surveillance mode. This also enabled it to analyse the interior architecture of buildings, monitor radio transmissions and phone calls, and hack into computers.

A second vehicle, KARR (Knight Automated Roving Robot), was built to similar specifications, although it was deactivated and placed in storage. When it was accidentally reactivated, KARR went rogue and had to be destroyed by Michael and KITT.

In 1991, a follow-up movie, Knight Rider 2000, introduced the Knight 4000. The car was based on a Dodge Stealth but modified to look like a 1988 Pontiac Banshee Concept Car. It was hoped that this new vehicle would take over from KITT and would lead to a revamping of the series but this never materialised. Then in 2008 a Ford Shelby GT500KR was given a makeover for a TV series. The latest version of KITT (Knight Industries Three Thousand) had all the usual refinements and more, and it was hoped that a new series would be commissioned. Based on the life of Michael's estranged son, Michael Traceur (Justin Bruening), and featuring Val Kilmer as KITT, the

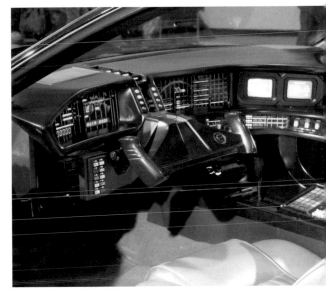

Above: *KITT's futuristic interior*

series only lasted for the TV movie and 17 episodes before being axed.

The original KITT remains one of the most famous cars in television history. Of the 23 Trans Ams that were used during filming, only one was beyond repair when the series finished in 1986. All except five of the remaining 22 were then dismantled. These five are now thought to be in private collections and theme parks, with two in the UK and three in the US.

The General Lee from The Dukes of Hazzard

The Dukes of Hazzard was an American action series focusing on the exploits of Bo and Luke Duke (John Schneider and Tom Wopat respectively), their beautiful cousin Daisy (Catherine Bach) and Uncle Jesse (Denver Pyle). They were constantly in trouble with the law, particularly crooked County Commissioner Jefferson Davis 'Boss' Hogg (Sorrell Booke) and his inept sheriffs, notably Rosco P Coltrane (James Best), Cletus Hogg (Rick Hurst) and Enos Strate (Sonny Shroyer).

The Duke Boys' car proved one of the most popular aspects of the show, and it has since become one of the most recognisable vehicles ever to appear on screen. The orange Dodge Charger (models were used from 1968-1970) had the Confederate battle flag painted on the roof (the army was commanded by General Robert E Lee) and its horn played the first 12 notes of the song *Dixie*. As the car performed outrageous stunts and jumps in almost every episode, at least 250 and probably more than 300 were used during the show's six-year run. (Only around 17 still exist, although several of these still carry battle scars from their stunt work.)

The cars were powered by a mix of 318, 383 or 440-cubic-inch Magnum V8 engines producing up to 375 horsepower. Cars that had to perform especially delicate stunt driving, on the side wheels for example, used the smaller and lighter engines, while the cars that had to perform the biggest jumps used the larger and more powerful big-block engines. To balance the cars in flight, up to half a ton of sand had to be placed in the boot, but many of the landings bent the chassis

so these cars were immediately retired on safety grounds due to the structural damage.

Because of the high rate of attrition, finding usable stunt cars later in the series became extremely difficult. If the stock cars couldn't be repaired and new vehicles couldn't be sourced, the only solution was to use radio-controlled models, although the stars of the show were distinctly underwhelmed with the latter option.

Andre and Renaud Veluzat were charged with keeping the vehicles roadworthy but, when they were caught selling wrecked cars, Warner Brothers gave the job to Ken Fritz. When he too was fired, WB took over the work themselves. The series ran until 1985 but the car made a welcome comeback in the 1997 TV reunion movie and the 2005 film starring Seann William Scott and Johnny Knoxville. Around 25 Chargers were used for the Hollywood blockbuster.

Above: More than 300 General Lees were destroyed filming The Dukes of Hazzard

James Bond's Aston Martins, Lotus & BMWs

Although the James Bond of Fleming's books usually drove a Bentley, the character did get to drive a 1963 Aston Martin DB III in the novel *Goldfinger*. By the time the film was released the following year, Aston Martin had developed the DB5 so this was Bond's transport of choice. Eon Productions couldn't afford to buy one so Aston loaned them two, the original prototype and another standard car for stunt work, although both were then used for promotional tours and were billed as the most famous cars in the world.

Academy Award-winning special-effects designer John Stears created a car that had a tracking device, revolving number plates (valid all countries, according to Q), tyre slasher, forward-firing machineguns, smoke screen, bullet-proof shield and, most famously of all, an ejector seat. All of the gadgets were used by Sean Connery's Bond in the film and the car proved so popular that it reappeared in the pre-credits sequence for the next film, *Thunderball*, by which time rear-facing water cannon had also been added.

George Lazenby's Bond drove an Aston Martin DBS with a sniper rifle built into the glove compartment. As Roger Moore drove a gadget-laden Lotus, the Aston Martin brand didn't reappear in the Bond films until Timothy Dalton took the role in 1989's *The Living Daylights*. His V8 Vantage Volante also came with a hardtop as well as all the usual refinements: outriggers, spiked tyres, missiles, side-firing lasers and rocket propulsion. In the film, Bond escapes his pursuers across a frozen lake but then

crashes into a snowdrift. To avoid the car falling into enemy hands, he activates the self-destruct mechanism and completes his escape in a cello case!

Pierce Brosnan's Bond drove the original DB5 in *GoldenEye*'s opening car chase and it also made a brief appearance in *Tomorrow Never Dies*. It was also scheduled to appear in Scotland in *The World Is Not Enough* (1999) but these scenes were cut in the final edit. By his last outing as Bond in the totally over-the-

Above: *Arguably the most famous screen car of all time, James Bond's Aston Martin DB5 (with modifications)*

Above: *The modified Lotus Esprit from The Spy Who Loved Me*

top *Die Another Day* (2002), Brosnan was behind the wheel of the invisible Aston Martin Vanquish (Vanish). Although the chase sequence on the frozen lake in Iceland had its moments, the reliance on outrageous weaponry and poor CGI effects weakened the plot and detracted from the viewing experience.

In *Casino Royale* in 2006, Daniel Craig's Bond was seen to win the original DB5 in a game of poker, but later in the film he was at the wheel of the new DBS, which he then wrecked spectacularly. In *Quantum of Solace* he also drove the DBS, but he was back in the old DB5 during *Skyfall*, although this car was also destroyed at the film's climax.

The original DB5 lived up to its billing as the most famous car in the world when one of the two loaned to Eon for *Goldfinger* sold at auction for £2.6 million in 2010. The remaining prototype was stripped of its gadgets after filming and returned to Aston Martin. The company then sold it privately. The new owner refitted the weapons and other gadgets but the car was stolen in Florida in 1997 and is yet to be found. As it was the car with the ejector seat and not the one used primarily for general stunt work, it is believed to be considerably more valuable than the one sold at auction.

There's no doubt that Roger Moore's Bond's most famous car was the amphibious Lotus Esprit from *The Spy Who Loved Me*. Six vehicles were used in filming, although only one had the full submarine conversion. The interior for the amphibious car was merely a platform for two SCUBA divers and bore no resemblance to an actual road vehicle, however. After filming, the sub was placed in storage on Long Island in

New York. When the lease ran out after 10 years, no one claimed the contents so the locker was auctioned to buyers who didn't know what it contained. One lucky person paid just $100 for the iconic film prop, but they then exhibited the car over the next 24 years. This 'Wet Nellie' submersible version was sold to American businessman Elon Musk at auction in 2013 for £650,000. Musk has said that he wants to convert the Lotus to run on an electric motor before launching it as a proper submersible car.

Roger Moore's Bond also performed one of the most famous driving stunts in cinematic history in *The Man With The Golden Gun* (1974). While pursuing the villainous Scaramanga through the streets of Bangkok, Bond commandeers a red AMC Hornet hatchback from a car showroom. Although it appears that Scaramanga has escaped, Bond realises that he can still catch him if he can jump a watery creek. The only problem is that the bridge has fallen into disrepair and, having partially collapsed, doesn't span the width of the creek. The only way to make the jump is to drive the car up the spiral incline and perform a barrel roll before landing on the equally skewed off ramp.

Above: *Bond barrel rolls an AMC Hornet in The Man with the Golden Gun*

The stunt was originally designed by Raymond McHenry and W.J. Milligan, and tested at Cornell Aeronautical Laboratory in Buffalo, New York. When the computer factored in the weight of the car and driver and the 52-foot gap, a takeoff speed of 40mph was predicted. The corkscrew ramps were then set up and un-credited English driver Loren 'Bumps' Willard performed the stunt on the first take, for which he received an instant bonus of £30,000. The car is now in the National Motor Museum in Beaulieu in Hampshire. (Scaramanga eventually made his escape in a flying AMC Matador Coupe, which could actually take to the air for short flights.)

Timothy Dalton briefly used the Aston Martin Volante, but BMW then became the main car brand for Brosnan's 007 films. Although he drove a Z3 Roadster in the film *GoldenEye*, none of the gadgets described by Q (ejector seat, parachute-braking system and Stinger missiles) were

actually used. On the other hand, the 750iL driven by Bond in the dramatic car chase around a multi-storey car park in *Tomorrow Never Dies* deployed most of its gadgets to great effect: missiles, caltrops (metal tacks used to deflate the tyres of pursuing cars) and an impregnable body shell were enough to see off most of the villains, and Bond was also able to drive via remote control from his telephone.

BMW's association with the franchise ended with the Z8 in *The World Is Not Enough*. The car could drive itself and downed a helicopter with a missile, but it was then cut in half by a second helicopter fitted with a large blade attachment.

Above: *Daniel Craig's Bond drove an Aston Martin DBS in Quantum of Solace*

The A-Team's Van

The A-Team was an American action series that ran for 98 episodes between 1983 and 1987. It followed the lives of four ex-special forces veterans who were on the run from the military after being branded criminals for war crimes they didn't commit. Now mercenaries working for private individuals, they

solve crimes and bring local hoods to justice. Led by Colonel John 'Hannibal' Smith (George Peppard), the team also comprises Lieutenant Templeton Peck (Dirk Benedict), 'Howling Mad' Murdock (Dwight Schultz) and Sergeant Bosco Albert 'B.A.' Baracus (Lawrence 'Mr. T' Tureaud).

The team's preferred mode of transport was a 1983 GMC G-15 Vandura van with a 6.2-litre diesel V8. It is a commonly held misconception that the van was black, and almost all of the toys produced afterwards went with the single colour, when in fact the section above the characteristic red stripe was metallic grey. With its roof spoiler and red turbine mag wheels it has since become an icon of popular culture. The van contained a mini printing press, surveillance equipment and all of the disguises used by the team.

The DeLorean from Back to the Future

Back to the Future is a science-fiction comedy starring Michael J Fox as Marty McFly and Christopher Lloyd as crackpot inventor Doc Emmett Brown. Eccentric genius Doc Brown builds a time machine out of a DeLorean DMC-12 but he is then killed by Libyans from whom he stole the plutonium that powers the car. Marty escapes in the DeLorean but, during the pursuit, he hits the magical 88mph limit which triggers the time circuits and sends him from 1985 back to 1955. Without any plutonium to make the return leap through time, Marty is stranded in 1955.

Despite becoming the object of his mother's affections, he manages to introduce his parents to one another and then convince the young Doc Brown to help him channel a bolt of lightning into the DoLorean's flux capacitor – the instrument that makes time-travel possible – thereby providing enough power to send Marty back to the future. The film was a huge critical and commercial success and spawned two sequels, but the DeLorean ended up being the unlikely star.

John DeLorean convinced celebrities and then the Northern Ireland Development Agency to stump up the £175 million required to put the car – designed by Giorgetto Giugiaro – into production but it ended up being the only model produced by the company because the car market slumped in the early 1980s and it was only in production for two years. DeLorean himself made a number of unwise business investments and was then arrested on suspicion of drug trafficking, although he was later found not guilty.

Above: *The DeLorean DMC-12 from Back to the Future*

The company couldn't survive the scandal, however, and despite numerous technical innovations, as well as a rear-mounted engine, gull-wing doors and unpainted stainless-steel body panels that gave it a unique and desirable look, only 9,200 cars made it off the production line.

Six chassis were used while filming *Back to the Future*, while a single fibreglass version was built for the scenes were the car had to fly. One was destroyed at the end of the third film instalment, two were left to rot and the fibreglass replica was sold for scrap. Universal Studios salvaged two of the remaining cars, and they are occasionally put on show or used for promotional work, while the last is in a private collection.

Magnum's Ferrari

Magnum was a crime drama from the pens of Donald Bellisario and Glen Larson, whose credits also included *Airwolf*, *Quantum Leap*, *JAG* and *NCIS*. It followed the exploits of Thomas Magnum (played by Tom Selleck), a former naval officer and SEAL Team sniper who served with distinction in the Vietnam War. His final posting was with the Office of Naval Intelligence, although he resigned after 10 years having become disillusioned with military life. He then embarked on a career as a private investigator on the Hawaiian island of Oahu.

In many ways, Magnum seemed to have the perfect lifestyle: he lived in a luxury beach-house, drove his boss's red Ferrari 308 (one of the most iconic screen cars of all time), and was usually surrounded by a bevy of beautiful women.

The car used in the initial series was a Pininfarina-styled 1979 Ferrari 308GTS with a removable targa roof panel. It was powered by a double overhead cam 2.9-litre V8 with four Weber carburettors that developed 240 horsepower (slightly less than the European version which wasn't fitted with a catalytic converter). At the end of each season, the car was auctioned off and a new one was ordered for the subsequent series. (Most are now in private collections or museums.) In seasons 2-3 Magnum drove a 308GTSi and by 1982 he was in a 308 GTSi QV (quattrovalvole – four valves per cylinder). This version had a slim louvered panel to aid air circulation, electric door mirrors, new radiator grille, rectangular sidelights, heavier front bumpers and a deeper front spoiler.

All the cars used in the series had

their interiors modified because Selleck was 6'4". Padding was usually removed from the front seats and they were then bolted further back. There was a dedicated action car for the chases and other driving sequences, several kit car replicas (built on Pontiac Fiero chassis) for when cars needed to be destroyed or badly damaged, as well as another for the close-up shots.

The Green Hornet's Black Beauty

The Green Hornet was a masked vigilante who fought crime on American radio and TV shows. The character was created by George Trendle, Fran Striker and director James Jewell in 1936. By day, the character was Britt Reid, a wealthy publisher, but at night he pulled on a green overcoat and mask. The public believed the Green Hornet to be a villain, but this allowed him and his sidekick Kato to infiltrate the city's underworld and bring criminals to justice.

The series began life on the radio and in a series of comics but he graduated to the big screen with two movie serials in the early 1940s. It reached a wider audience when Van Williams became the Green Hornet and Bruce Lee became Kato in the ABC television adaptation in 1966. The car used in the series was a 1966 Imperial Crown that was modified by Dean Jeffries for around $50,000. It fired explosives from tubes below the headlights, had a gas nozzle in the front grille, infra-green lights and could launch a remote controlled surveillance device from the boot. The main car used during filming was bought by Dan Goodman for $10,000 in 1992. He asked Jeffries to restore it and it is now part of the Petersen Automotive Museum Collection. A second car from the series is in a private collection in South Carolina.

Another series of comics appeared in 1989, and this was when the original cars were transformed into Black Beauty, at first a Pontiac Banshee and then a 1998 Oldsmobile Touring Sedan. In 2009 Dynamite Entertainment acquired the rights to produce another series of comics,

although DC Comics suggested doing a crossover with Batman in 2014.

In 2006, French director Aurélien Poitrimoult released a short film about the character (Universal and Miramax had both been discussing a Hollywood version but nothing had come of it so far).

Then, in 2011, Columbia Pictures released a feature film starring Seth Rogen. His car, the latest incarnation of Black Beauty, was a 1964 Imperial Crown sedan. It was equipped with two Browning machineguns, Stinger missiles, a flamethrower, shotguns, anti-riot spikes and modified door guns. Only three of the 29 cars used during filming survived intact, with the rest being destroyed while on stunt duty.

The Fall Guy's Truck

The Fall Guy was an American action/adventure series that ran from 1981 until 1986. It starred Lee Majors as stuntman Colt Seavers, Douglas Barr as his cousin, sidekick and stuntman-in-training Howie Munson, and the gorgeous Heather Thomas as Jody Banks. Seavers wasn't particularly well paid in the movie business so he also moonlighted as a bounty hunter bringing fugitives to justice.

His transport of choice was a 1982 GMC K-2500 Wideside truck with Sierra Grande modifications, although a similar K-25 was also used in filming. It had 4-inch Burbank suspension and enormous 36-inch Dick Cepek off-road tyres. It also had a custom roll bar and grille, a winch and a secret compartment that Seavers used to stash weapons or hide criminals.

The trucks performed numerous jumps and stunt driving sequences and the rate of attrition was reasonably high (in the opening credits, for example, the truck leaping over a guard rail onto a highway clearly breaks its front axle). Models with different headlight configurations and bed lengths meant that inconsistencies crept into the shows, although most of the trucks were powered by stock 350-cubic-inch turbo V8s.

As more succumbed to the rigours of filming, a dedicated stunt truck was built with a reinforced frame, heavy-duty axles, dual shocks, upgraded suspension and counterweights in the bed, and a mid-mounted engine to provide balance during the jumps. When the series was axed in 1986, the remaining trucks were auctioned or given away in competitions.

The Saint's Jaguar XJ-S and Volvo P1800

The Saint began life as a detective series that gradually morphed into a spy thriller in the James Bond mould. Novelist Leslie Charteris created the character of Simon Templar –his initials explain how the name of his alter ego was derived – in the 1920s. Roger Moore had always expressed a desire to play the part if the books were ever adapted for the screen, and he actually tried to acquire the rights himself. Before he became co-owner of the show with Robert Baker, he had been asked to try for the part.

The Saint introduced a number of props, such as the iconic white Volvo P1800, and also broke the 'fourth wall' in that Moore often addressed the audience directly. Cubby Broccoli and Harry Saltzman were so impressed with his performance that they repeatedly tried to lure him to the big screen to play James Bond, but Moore was tied to the series and felt that Connery was still the right man for the job.

The original white Volvo P1800 had a troubled history: Volvo's previous sports car (the P1900) had been a disaster and only 68 were sold. Pelle Petterson of Italian automotive engineers Pietro Frua designed the P1800. Three prototypes were built in 1957 but Volvo couldn't find backers to finance the project until after they'd unveiled the car at the 1960 Brussels Motor Show. British company Jensen agreed to take on the manufacturing and assembly in Birmingham and the first cars rolled off the production line in 1960.

The show's producers initially approached Jaguar in the hope that the company would lend them one of

the new E-Types, but Jaguar declined because they had a long waiting list already and didn't need further exposure. The other car that caught their attention at the 1961 Geneva Motor Show was the P1800 and Volvo were only too happy to supply two for the series, one for studio shots and close-ups and one for external action sequences. The Saint's car was a 1962 model with the number plate ST1

and Roger Moore loved the car so much that he bought one for himself.

When Moore eventually took the role of 007 it seemed as if audiences had seen the last of the Saint, but Ian Ogilvy brought Simon Templar back to the small screen in 1978. The latest incarnation only lasted 24 episodes, however, although it did introduce a new car to audiences in the shape of a white Jaguar XJ-S.

Del Trotter's Van

Only Fools and Horses was a British sitcom based on the lives and exploits of Peckham's most famous sons: Derek (Del Boy) and Rodney Trotter, their granddad and Uncle Albert. Del Boy, played by David Jason, was a dodgy market trader who lost more money than he ever earned, Rodney (Nicholas Lyndhurst) was his long-suffering younger brother, while granddad (Lennard Pearce) and Albert (Buster Merryfield) completed the multi-generation line-up (the brothers' estranged father also turned up in one episode).

The Trotters' 1973 yellow Reliant Regal Supervan has become a star in its own right and has certainly achieved cult status via its exposure on the BBC. The one most often used on set was part of the Cars of the Stars Museum in Keswick, Cumbria, but it is now part of an exhibition at the National Motor Museum in Beaulieu. Others belong in private collections. Boxer Ricky Hatton bought one in 2004 and another was sold at auction for £44,000 in 2007. As six were apparently used during filming, another three must still exist. The logo on the side panel advertises Trotters Independent Trading Company of New York, Paris and Peckham, although despite the (mostly) glamorous locations, the tax disc was always in the post and the van was in desperate need of repair.

The Regal itself was a small three-wheeled van that was manufactured in Tamworth between 1953 and 1973. The first incarnation used a wooden sub-frame but by 1962 it had a steel chassis, bonded shell and 600cc OHV Reliant engine

producing 25bhp. Later versions used a 747cc engine that boosted power to 35bhp, as well as incorporating glass–fibre body panels to save weight and increase structural rigidity. Although the vehicles occasionally received bad press for their instability and small load capacity, they have become an iconic screen machine after serving the Trotters for more than 20 years.

Above: *Del and Rodney's Reliant Regal was usually in a state of disrepair*

Mr Bean's Mini

Rowan Atkinson's Mr Bean may only have appeared in 14 episodes of the sitcom but the character has become one of the most widely known comic creations in the world. Indeed the show has been sold to 245 territories and achieved a record audience of 18.74 million for the 1991 episode *The Trouble with Mr Bean*. The character himself rarely speaks so the humour is largely physical and usually revolves around Mr Bean's interaction with other people or how he solves trivial problems in unusual ways. He is a juvenile buffoon who seems blissfully unaware of how things work, but he always manages to make the absurd believable and has become one of the most endearing characters on television.

Mr Bean's first car was an orange 1969 British Motor Corporation Mini Mark II but this was crashed off-screen after the first episode. Thereafter the character drove a green 1976 British Leyland Mini 1000, which, over the course of the five-year run the series enjoyed, became something of a star in its own right. It had several innovative security measures, such as being locked with a bolt latch and padlock, and Mr Bean often removed the steering wheel instead of the key.

When the series ended in 1995 the cars, other than making brief cameos in the 1997 film *Bean*, were sold. One went to Kariker Kars and was then hired out for events, another ended up in the Cars of the Stars Motor Museum (this closed in 2011, after which most of the vehicles were sold to American collectors), one is being restored in the UK and a couple of replicas are also in circulation. Another was bought by the National Motor Museum at Beaulieu in Hampshire.

Automan's Lamborghini Countach LP400

Opposite:
*Automan's
Lamborghini*

Automan was a science-fiction/superhero series from the pen of Glen Larson (*Battlestar Galactica*, *The Fall Guy* and *Knight Rider*, amongst others). Larson's premise was that police officer and computer programmer Walter Nebicher (played by Desi Arnaz) had created an artificial life-form in his hard drive. The entity could then leave the program at night and come to life as a hologram (Chuck Wagner) to fight crime. His sidekick, Cursor, was a shape-shifting polyhedron that could create physics-defying objects like supercars or aircraft.

The Autocar was a Lamborghini Countach LP400 that could corner and overtake at high speeds and generate extreme g-forces. The original Countach was styled by inexperienced designer Marcello Gandini of Bertone.

What he lacked in experience he made up for in innovation and he produced a stunning shape. The car was wide and low but also relatively short, and it had trapezoidal panels. The doors were also hinged at the front to open upwards. With each incarnation, the styling was adjusted for practical, ergonomic and economical reasons but the initial LP400 remains one of the most beautiful supercars ever built. It was powered by a mid-mounted 4-litre V12 producing 375bhp. With a curb weight of only a ton, it was apparently capable of 0-60mph in 5.4 seconds and a top speed of 192mph.

Although the *Automan* premise was unusual, the series was expected to catch on via its interesting hook. Only 13 episodes were made, however, and ABC axed it after a single season (1983-4).

The Pontiac Firebird Trans Am from Smokey and the Bandit

Smokey and the Bandit was a 1977 film about bootlegging beer across America. Texans Big Enos Burdette (Pat McCormick) and son Little Enos (Paul Williams) are looking for a truck driver who will transport 400 cases of beer from Texas to the Southern Classic in Georgia. Legendary driver Bo 'Bandit' Darville (Burt Reynolds) accepts the challenge and enlists big-rig driver Cledus 'Snowman' Snow (Jerry Reed) to take the wheel of the truck while he distracts the law in his Pontiac Trans Am.

The pair run into numerous problems with the cops, particularly Sheriff Buford T Justice (Jackie Gleason) and his dim-witted son Junior (Mike Henry). Indeed most of the remainder of the film revolves around the action sequences where Bandit repeatedly escapes while the Smokeys (police) crash their squad cars before resuming the chase.

The Pontiac Firebird entered production in 1967 but second-generation cars (1970-81) appeared in the film. Although these cars had a variety of engines from 231-cubic-inch (3.8-litre) V6s to 455-cubic-inch 7.5-litre 366bhp V8s, the ones in the film were severely under-powered and could only put out around 200bhp. Special editions were released to coincide with the original film and its sequels.

Four modified 1976 Trans Ams were used during filming *Smokey and the Bandit*, and all were damaged during shooting, particularly in the jump scenes. In the stunt where Bandit leaps over a gap in a dismantled bridge, the car was completely destroyed. Pontiac also supplied two LeMans cars, which were also severely damaged. By the time the

shoot was complete, only one of each was still running, while the others had all been cannibalised for parts.

Burt Reynolds was the top box-office star at the time and, despite only having a budget of around $4 million and being directed by stuntman Hal Needham rather than a recognised industry professional, the film became a huge commercial success. It eventually grossed $300 million worldwide and was the second biggest film of 1977 after *Star Wars*. Its success

prompted the production team to release a sequel in 1980. With a bigger budget of $17 million it was expected to do even better but the formula was already tiring (it had been preceded by *The Gumball Rally* and would be imitated by *The Cannonball Run*) and it only limped to $66 million. A second sequel in 1983 was a complete flop, although by then Reynolds had wisely jumped ship. Thankfully the fabulous car remained popular and is still in the public consciousness today.

Above: *The 1976 Pontiac Firebird Trans Am from Smokey and the Bandit*

The 1959 Miller-Meteor Cadillac from Ghostbusters

Ghostbusters was an American supernatural comedy about three phoney parapsychologists – Peter Venkman (Bill Murray), Ray Stantz (Dan Aykroyd) and Egon Spengler (Harold Ramis) – who suddenly realise that a series of paranormal events is linked to a portal to the spirit world. When they are sacked from their positions at Columbia University they form Ghostbusters, an outfit whose equipment is suitable for capturing and storing ghosts and ghouls. With spirit activity in New York mushrooming, they suddenly become the men of the moment: celebrity ghost catchers.

They blast around town in the Ghostbusters car – Ecto 1 – which was a 1959 Cadillac Futura hearse/ambulance with a red-and-white colour scheme. The vehicle was bought for $4,800 but it is in a poor state of repair and needs, according to Stantz: suspension work and shocks, brakes, brake pads, a steering box, transmission, new rings, mufflers and a little wiring. The team quickly restores the vehicle so that it's roadworthy and can store their proton packs, radar, various detectors and sensors, and a microwave satellite uplink. (For the sequel, the car was upgraded with more technical equipment and digital advertising boards on the roof.)

The original movie was a huge hit, returning receipts of nearly $300 million on a budget of $30 million. It was nominated for Academy Awards for Best Visual Effects (although it lost out to *Indiana Jones and the Temple of Doom*) and Best Original Song for Ray Parker Junior's *Ghostbusters* theme (it lost to the title track for *The Woman in Red*). Critics

and audiences gave it overwhelmingly favourable reviews, with the car listed as a highlight.

The first incarnation makes regular celebrity appearances at *Ghostbusters*-related events, while the car used in the sequel is currently being restored by Sony. (The second film wasn't as popular but still generated a box-office take of $215 million.) One car purportedly to be one of the three originals used in the first film attracted bids up to $45,000 on eBay but, as this didn't reach the reserve, the car went unsold. It was later rumoured to be a replica rather than one of the originals, all of which are apparently still at Universal Studios. Faithful representations of the originals can attract prices as high as £70,000.

The Pontiac Firebird Esprit from The Rockford Files

The Rockford Files was an American drama from the creative team of novelist and screenwriter Roy Huggins (*Maverick*, *The Fugitive*) and prolific producer Stephen Cannell (*The A-Team*, *Hardcastle and McCormick*). The character of Jim Rockford was written for James Garner, with the actor given licence to play a detective in the Maverick mould but updated for a contemporary series set in Malibu, California. Unlike most private investigators of that generation, Rockford avoided physical confrontation, rarely carried his Colt Special revolver, and invariably worked cold cases to save conflicting with active police investigations.

Rockford drove a gold Pontiac Firebird Esprit, with which he pioneered the evasive driving manoeuvre known as a J-turn, whereby the car is thrown into reverse, spun to face the opposite direction using the steering wheel and footbrake or emergency brake, and then crammed into first gear to complete the getaway. Garner claimed that he performed this stunt throughout the series' 130-episode six-year run. Stuntman Royden Clark did the remainder of the driving.

Garner had actually learned to drive seriously for the 1966 film *Grand Prix*, in which several Formula 1 drivers also made appearances. For everyone's safety, the actors had to be qualified stunt drivers so Garner learned his craft and earned acceptance from the other stars. By the time he was cast in *The Rockford Files*, he was an accomplished off-road racer and stunt driver.

The car itself was regularly updated during filming, beginning with the

1974 Esprit and ending with a 1978 Formula 400S that was modified to look like an Esprit. It was the base model of the Pontiac portfolio but that fit nicely with the character's down-on-his-luck image. The engines were all from higher-end cars, however, with three vehicles being used per season. Several of the originals are now in the collection of Patrick McKinney.

Above: *The Pontiac Firebird Esprit from The Rockford Files*

Hardcastle and McCormick's 1971 Volkswagen Coyote

Hardcastle and McCormick was an American action/drama series from Stephen Cannell (*Ironside, Columbo, The A-Team*) and Patrick Hasburgh (*21 Jump Street, SeaQuest 2032*). It ran on the ABC network for 67 episodes from 1983 until 1986 and starred Brian Keith as Judge Milton Hardcastle and Daniel Kelly as ex-con and stunt driver Mark 'Skid' McCormick.

Hardcastle was an eccentric judge who decided after retiring that he would hunt down the criminals who had escaped justice in his court. Mark McCormick was a streetwise car thief who recently 'procured' the prototype Coyote X sportscar after its designer and owner (his friend) was murdered. Instead of putting McCormick away for the theft, Hardcastle struck a deal with him whereby they would try to catch the killer. McCormick would then be allowed to keep the car providing he continued to work as the judge's agent.

The car, of course, ended up being the star of the series. The Coyote X was built loosely on the design of a McLaren M6GT, the road-going version of the M6A Can-Am race-car that was developed by New Zealand Formula 1 driver Bruce McLaren. The body panels were made from custom moulds and then assembled by Mike Fennel. Although the front section remained faithful to the McLaren, the rear quarter was custom built and became a stock part for Manta Montage kit cars. The main differences between the Coyotes and the Mantas were the wheel wells and shape of the boot.

The chassis for the car used in the first season came from a Volkswagen Beetle, while the engine was from a Porsche 914. (The 2-litre unit only produced around

110bhp so the performance was nothing like what viewers would have expected given the outrageous styling.) Thereafter the Coyote was modelled on the DeLorean DMC-12 with a wider front end because Brian Keith found it difficult to get in and out of the original car.

A series-one car is now in the hands of a private collector in New Jersey, while the stunt car was upgraded for the pilot of *Knight Rider 2000* and then turned into Jay Ohrberg's show car. Ohrberg, a designer and collector of exotic screen cars, then sold the car in 2011 to another collector in Texas who intends to return it to the original Coyote specification.

Above: *The extraordinary Volkswagen Coyote from Hardcastle and McCormick*

Mad Max's customised 1973 Ford Falcon XB Interceptor

Mad Max was a low-budget apocalyptic Australian action/thriller that starred Mel Gibson as he tracked down the gang that murdered his wife and child. Max Rockatansky was formerly an officer with the Main Force Patrol who was trying to maintain law and order as society broke down in the wake of fuel crises and energy shortages. With many of his colleagues dead and his family murdered, Max took matters into his own hands and slipped behind the wheel of the MFP's most fearsome car, a supercharged black Ford XB Falcon Interceptor Pursuit Special. (This wasn't the first car he used in the film – that was a modified Holden Monaro – but it was the more memorable of the two.)

The car began life as a white 1973 GT Coupe but, when producers Byron Kennedy and George Miller saw one, they hired Murray Smith to turn it into the Pursuit Special. His team modified the nose, added side exhaust pipes and cut a hole in the bonnet for a (non-functioning) supercharger.

The success of the first film prompted producers to make a sequel, *Mad Max 2: The Road Warrior*. Kennedy and Miller's production team modified the car further, changing the rear wheels, supercharger and exhaust system. It also had extra fuel tanks fitted to the boot and appeared to be in a much more dishevelled state. The story involved destroying the car so a replica was blown up instead. The original was restored after filming before being sold to the Cars of the Stars Museum in Keswick, Cumbria. When the museum closed in 2011 most of the exhibits were sold to private collectors and the iconic Falcon XB Interceptor is now in the

Dezer Car Museum in Miami.

A fourth instalment of the film was expected to follow *Mad Max: Beyond Thunderdome* but it spent a quarter of a century in development hell and Mel Gibson eventually lost interest. Miller then announced in 2003 that a script had been finalised and a budget of $100 million had been agreed with Warner Brothers. The project was shelved again over security concerns and travel restrictions during the war on terror but it finally began filming in Namibia in 2012. Reshoots delayed the release but it should hit screens in 2015. As the story is set before the first film, the original Falcon made a comeback and can be expected to play a major role in the new release.

Above: *The Ford Falcon Interceptor from Mad Max*

The AMC Pacer from Wayne's World

Wayne's World was an American comedy starring Mike Myers as Wayne Campbell and Dana Carvey as Garth Algar respectively. The two layabout rockers host their own cable TV show in Aurora, Illinois, but, when they are noticed by a major network, they agree to sign over the rights to the show. Little realising they are being exploited by the network, the pair eventually find themselves battling to save their show (in between attending gigs).

While returning from one rock show, the pair and their entourage are seen driving the 'Mirth Mobile', a blue 1976 AMC Pacer with decal flames down the sides. AMC produced Pacers between 1975 and 1980, although they were basic little cars that only produced 90 horsepower. A V8 version did make it off the production line but there was a fuel crisis in the late '70s so there was little demand for a gas-guzzler.

Garth's Pacer had a liquorice dispenser mounted on the headliner and a beer tap installed on the dashboard above the glove box. It initially only had a radio/cassette deck but, when the pair got their big break, Garth splashed out on a CD player. The car also had mismatched wheels and tyres.

The film also starred Tia Carrere, Rob Lowe, Meat Loaf and Alice Cooper and was a big commercial success, returning nearly $200 million on a $20 million budget. The following year's sequel had an all-star cast, with the likes of Christopher Walken, Kim Basinger, Charlton Heston, Drew Barrymore and Aerosmith all making appearances. Despite generally positive reviews, the film couldn't recapture the quirky genius of the original and stiff competition from *Mrs Doubtfire* and *Schindler's List* ensured it was a comparative failure at the box office.

Thelma and Louise's Ford Thunderbird

Thelma and Louise is an adventure thriller from director Ridley Scott. Thelma (Geena Davis) and Louise (Susan Sarandon) take a road trip into the mountains so they can escape their controlling husband and dull waitress job respectively. The trip soon takes a dark turn as Louise shoots a man who tries to rape Thelma after a night in a bar. As fugitives they go on the run and spend the rest of the film evading the police and racking up the body count.

They head for Mexico in their convertible Ford Thunderbird until they are finally cornered by the police on the rim of the Grand Canyon. Rather than surrender to the authorities, Louise floors the accelerator and drives the Thunderbird off the cliff.

The car used in the film was a blue-green 1966 convertible with a 390-cubic-inch (6.4-litre) V8 developing 315bhp, although versions with a 428-cubic-inch (7-litre) 345bhp engine did appear later that year. One of the five cars used in filming was sold at an Italian auction in 2008 for $65,000. It seems that the remaining four slipped into obscurity after the film finished shooting.

The Lamborghini Countach LP400S from The Cannonball Run

The Cannonball Run was a 1981 film about a madcap road race across America. Inspired by the exploits of, and then written by, Brock Yates, the movie was directed by renowned stuntman Hal Needham and starred a host of big names from Burt Reynolds and Roger Moore to Farrah Fawcett, Jackie Chan, Dean Martin and Sammy Davis Jr.

JJ McClure (Reynolds) and Victor Prinzim (Dom DeLuise) drove a Dodge Tradesman ambulance so they could avoid traffic jams and wouldn't be suspected by the police (this was the actual vehicle used by Yates during his famous cross-country dash in 1971). The McClure role had been written for Steve McQueen but the actor had just been diagnosed with cancer so Reynolds was chosen instead.

A host of other teams and drivers rolled up to the start in Connecticut, although cops galore and Mr Arthur J Foyt (named after Indianapolis 500 legend A.J. Foyt), a representative from the Safety Enforcement Unit, were on hand to stop them competing. Each team had a method for evading capture, with Jackie Chan's Mitsubishi team (which was actually a Subaru) capable of becoming a version of Knight Rider's KITT, and Roger Moore's Aston Martin DB5 using all of James Bond's gadgets (even though his character's name was Seymour Goldfarb). Jackie Chan and engineer Michael Hui also brought their martial arts to the fore when fighting Henry Fonda's gang of bikers.

Although it didn't get much screen time, the most striking car used in the film was a black series two Lamborghini Countach LP400S with the iconic 3.9-litre 375bhp V12. It was driven by

Marcie Thatcher (played by Adrienne Barbeau) and Jill Rivers (Tara Buckman), who used their sex appeal – they wore figure-hugging one-piece spandex outfits for the entire film – to talk their way out of tricky situations. It had an extra front bumper added to conform with US automobile legislation, as well as 12 exhaust pipes. It was owned by Hawaiian Tropic until 2008 when it was sold to a private collector for complete restoration.

In the 1984 sequel, Jill and Marcie were played by Susan Anton and Catherine Bach. Their Lamborghini started off white but, when they were pursued by the police during the opening credits, they pulled over and had the paint washed off to reveal a red coat underneath. While the first Cannonball proved a surprise hit with moviegoers, the second completely bombed and it became the last film in this formula for Burt Reynolds.

Above: *The Countach was one of the most exciting cars of the 1970s*

Austin Powers's E-Type 'Shaguar'

Austin Powers was the comic creation of Mike Myers (*Wayne's World*). He appeared in three films, *Austin Powers: International Man of Mystery* (1997); *The Spy Who Shagged Me* (1999); and *Austin Powers in Goldmember* (2002). The character was a parody of James Bond and was probably inspired by Myers's father, television presenter Simon Dee and an amalgamation of several characters played by Peter Sellers.

Austin Powers needed to look cool at all times so his car was a Jaguar E-Type painted with Union Jack livery. The E-Type was first produced in 1961 and its stunning looks, keen price and high performance ensured it became an instant success. Indeed Enzo Ferrari remarked that it was the most beautiful car ever made. The series one used a six-cylinder 3.8-litre XK6 engine from the XK150S. In 1964, the capacity was increased to 4.2 litres, although power (265bhp) and top speed (150mph) remained unchanged. The car featured independent rear suspension, disc brakes all round, leather bucket seats, chrome-spoked wheels and a detachable hard top for the convertible.

Powers's series two 1970 4.2-litre Jaguar had its customised interior coloured red, white and blue. Several promotional left-hand-drive versions have cropped up on internet auctions but the original used in the film was right-hand-drive and remains in the Jaguar museum.

The AC Cobra and Ferrari 365GTB from The Gumball Rally

The plot for *The Gumball Rally* was inspired by the exploits of journalist Brock Yates who had himself drawn inspiration from Erwin 'Cannonball' Baker's coast-to-coast driving records across the United States. Yates then decided to organise a race from 'sea to shining sea', the first of which was run in 1971 (after he'd completed an exploratory crossing with a friend in a van).

Yates and his vastly experienced co-driver Dan Gurney won the first event in a Ferrari 365GTB/4 Daytona. They made the journey from New York to Los Angeles – a distance of 2,790 miles – in 35 hours and 53 minutes, thereby breaking the 55mph speed limit by an average of 22mph. The race was run five more times before being discontinued in 1979. Yates then wrote the screenplay for the film *The Cannonball Run*, which starred Burt Reynolds and was directed by experienced stuntman Hal Needham.

Having heard about Yates's trip, Charles Bail and Leon Capetanos penned a screenplay about an illegal road race across America. Michael Sarrazin was chosen to play Michael Bannon, while his co-driver in their blue AC Cobra was Professor Samuel Graves (played by Nicholas Pryor). Their main rivals were Steve Smith (Tim McIntire) and Franco Bertollini (Raúl Juliá) in a red Ferrari Daytona. Norman Burton provided the counterpoint as LAPD Lieutenant Roscoe, whose mission was to have the race cancelled and the drivers arrested.

Both cars remain among the most beautiful ever built. Original Cobras are rare and virtually priceless, while the Daytona was perhaps *the* iconic supercar of the late 1960s and early 1970s.

The Ferrari Testarossa and Daytona Spyder from Miami Vice

Miami Vice broke new ground in the 1980s and it has since become one of the most recognisable and influential police dramas in television history. A two-hour pilot based in South Florida about a pair of vice cops combating drug smuggling and prostitution was shown in 1985 and it proved extremely popular with audiences. The production team realised that they also had to appeal to the MTV generation so they used high-octane rock and pop music – particularly the pounding keyboards of Jan Hammer who wrote the theme tune – groundbreaking visual effects to drive the action, and a collection of iconic screen cars.

For the first couple of seasons, Detective James 'Sonny' Crockett (Don Johnson) drove a black 1975 Ferrari Daytona Spyder 365GTS/4,

although the actual car was a kit based on a 1980 Chevrolet Corvette C3. The modifications, which included fitting the new chassis with Ferrari-style body panels and trim, were carried out by bodywork specialists McBurnie. When Ferrari filed a lawsuit against McBurnie for manufacturing the replicas, the show's producers blew up the Daytona in the middle of the third season. Ferrari then had a change of heart and supplied the crew with two new Testarossas instead. They then built a third car to be used in the stunt scenes. It was based on the chassis of a De Tomaso Pantera, which had the same wheelbase as the Testarossa and so was perfect for swapping damaged panels.

Crockett's partner, Ricardo 'Rico' Tubbs (Philip Michael Thomas), clearly got the short straw because he

drove a 1964 Cadillac Coupe de Ville convertible. However, such was the popularity of the show that brands like Lamborghini, AMG, BMW, Maserati, DeLorean and Porsche all provided cars to be used by the stars.

The Minis from The Italian Job

The Italian Job was a British crime caper about a group of thieves who planned to steal $4 million dollars' worth of gold bullion from an armoured truck in Turin. Roger Beckermann (Rossano Brazzi) had originally planned the heist but the Mafia got wind of the plot and had him killed. His friend, Charlie Croker (Michael Caine), an East End gangster, was then given details of the scheme by Beckermann's widow. Croker saw the potential in the plan so set about recruiting a team to carry it out.

The armoured truck was scheduled to pass through Turin while England were playing Italy. This allowed most of the thieves to enter the city disguised as football fans. Croker's team then brought traffic to a standstill by hacking into the city's CCTV and traffic control systems. The thieves overpowered the guards and hijacked the truck, driving it through a prearranged route to the entrance hall of the Museo Egizio. The gold was then transferred to three Minis to complete the getaway through car parks, shopping arcades, back streets and even the city's sewer system while the police were still hampered by the gridlock.

The escape sequence with the red, white and blue Minis contains some of the most famous scenes in cinematic history. The manufacturer, the British Motor Corporation, only provided a handful of cars for the film so the producers had to buy 26 more at trade price. This almost led to them choosing Fiats instead, but the tone of the film and its distinct Britishness meant the Minis were retained. After filming had concluded, of the 16 Minis that had actually been used on-screen, only six survived. They were abandoned

in the garage in Turin that the crew had been using and neither Paramount nor the Oakhurst production team returned to collect them. If they still survive, their whereabouts are unknown but their value would be incalculable.

It should be noted that gold valued at $4 million in the late 1960s would have weighed more than three tons. Each Mini only weighed 630kg, or around 800kg with a driver and passenger, so it's extremely unlikely that they could have handled another ton of cargo each.

In 2003 a Hollywood remake (starring Mark Wahlberg as Croker) included a high-octane escape scene through Los Angeles with three new Mini Coopers. Although many critics panned the film, it wasn't really intended as a remake and was more of an homage, for which it deserves credit. The original received a Golden Globe nomination and was extremely popular in the UK. Indeed many of the catchphrases ("You're only supposed to blow the bloody doors off!") have entered the lexicon. The film wasn't marketed as effectively in the US and a sequel was shelved even though the original ended with the perfect cliffhanger.

Above: *The cars make their escape laden with gold bullion*

Bumblebee from Transformers

Transformers is a global entertainment franchise that was founded by the Japanese toy company Takara Tomy and the American organisation Hasbro in 1994. The latter took toys manufactured in Japan and turned them into gadgets that transformed into different shapes. Most of them began as cars, boats or aircraft that then metamorphosed into humanoid robots. They became an instant hit and were soon featuring in comics and on the big and small screen.

The first generation of toys appeared in the late 1980s, while the comics focused on the battle between the villainous Megatron and heroic Optimus Prime, both of whom had crash landed on a pre-historic Earth. The first animated television series aired in 1984 and ran for three years and 98 episodes. A cartoon movie based on the same characters was released in 1986, although it only just recouped its production costs at the box office. More comics and cartoons followed but it wasn't until Hollywood got its hands on the rights to make a feature film that the series was revitalised and reached a new generation of fans.

The character of Bumblebee was originally a small yellow autobot that masqueraded as a Volkswagen Beetle. He was smart and brave and his motivation was to impress Optimus Prime. The 2007 movie *Transformers* was produced by Steven Spielberg and directed by Michael Bay. In the film and subsequent sequels, the robot was disguised as a yellow Chevrolet Camaro instead because the Beetle reminded the production team of Herbie and they didn't want audiences making the same connection. Unlike many of the other robots, Bumblebee

was mute because his vocal processor had been damaged in a battle with Hardtop (in most preceding literature, the damage was actually caused by Megatron).

The first incarnation was a clapped out 1969 Camaro, although the producers then went for a model from 1977 with yellow and black stripes and a riveted bonnet scoop. In the transformation, the vehicle became a 2005 Camaro Concept Car (which was itself based on a Saleen Holden Monaro). The car was equipped with a plasma cannon and missile launchers, and in later films various trim parts and other accessories (such as new alloy wheels) were added. Indeed in *Transformers: Age of Extinction*, Bumblebee transforms into a 2014 Camaro Concept car. The vehicle plays a crucial role in the outcome of all four movies released to date.

The Ford Mustang and Dodge Charger from Bullitt

Bullitt is an American thriller starring Steve McQueen as Lieutenant Frank Bullitt, Robert Vaughn as politician Walter Chalmers and Jacqueline Bisset as Bullitt's girlfriend Cathy. With Chalmers investigating organised crime, he plans to present a witness to a senate subcommittee hearing in San Francisco. Bullitt is assigned to protect the witness but while another officer is on duty the witness and protection officer are attacked by hitmen. Bullitt eventually locates the assassins and so begins one of the most iconic car chases in film history.

With Bullitt at the wheel of a dark green 1968 Ford Mustang GT and their quarry in a Dodge Charger R/T, the cars screech around the streets of San Francisco. The scene begins in the Fisherman's Wharf area and lasts 11 minutes before ending with Bullitt forcing the Charger off the road into a petrol station on the Guadalupe Parkway outside the city.

Two 325bhp Mustang GT 390 V8 Fastbacks with four-speed manual transmissions were used during shooting, both of which were lent to the production team by Ford in exchange for promotional appearances. Car racer Max Balchowsky modified the engines, suspension and brakes so that the cars could cope with the rigours of stunt work over a three-week shooting schedule. Multiple camera angles were used so that the footage could then be edited into a montage that included the view from the drivers' perspectives as well as from the roadside.

McQueen was already an accomplished stunt driver so he did most of the close-up work. Bud Ekins and

Loren Janes then drove the car for the high-speed shots and the more dangerous stunts. Veteran stuntman Bill Hickman, meanwhile, played the part of one of the hitmen, drove the Dodge Charger and coordinated much of the completed scene. The Dodge 440 was a much more powerful car so the drivers had to balance their speeds constantly otherwise it would have pulled away from the Mustang. Speeds were supposed to be limited to 80mph on safety grounds but the drivers regularly reported hitting 110mph on the wider streets. Frank Keller won the Academy Award for Best Film Editing

in 1968 purely for his work on the groundbreaking sequence, and the car chase has since been voted the greatest in cinema history.

One of the Mustangs was scrapped at the end of the film because it had sustained so much damage. The second was sold to a Warner Brothers employee. It then changed hands several times – even McQueen tried to buy it at one point – but its whereabouts are now uncertain. Rumour has it that the car is in a private collection somewhere in the Ohio River Valley. In 2001 Ford released a *Bullitt* anniversary edition of the Mustang GT.

Above: *Steve McQueen at the wheel during the groundbreaking car chase in Bullitt*

The Plymouth Fury from Christine

Christine was an American horror film based on the Stephen King novel of the same name. Directed by John Carpenter and starring Keith Gordon as Arnie Cunningham and John Stockwell as his school friend Dennis Guilder, the 1983 film also starred a sentient and malevolent 1958 Plymouth Fury.

Arnie bought the ruined car in order to restore it but, as soon as he had completed the Fury's restoration (during which time he developed from shy nerd into a cocky kid who was increasingly popular with the ladies), his nemesis at school, Buddy Repperton (William Ostrander), and his gang wrecked it one night in a fit of jealous rage. When Arnie discovered the car he was distraught but he then noticed

that the Fury, nicknamed Christine, could actually repair itself. Christine then came to life and hunted down the gang members who had destroyed her. (The number plate CQB241 supposedly alludes to the military term for close-quarter battle.)

In King's novel the car was possessed by the spirit of a former owner, but the film makes it clear that it was evil from the moment it left the showroom. Two other Plymouth models were used during filming, the Belvedere and the Savoy, because original Furys were rare and expensive and were only released with a beige colour scheme. Only two cars of around 20 bought by the production team still exist. One was found in a junkyard and restored by Bill Gibson. He now exhibits the car at shows across the country.

The Ferrari 250GT California Spyder from Ferris Bueller's Day Off

Ferris Bueller's Day Off is a film about a slacker (Matthew Broderick) and the single eventful day that he takes off school. Director John Hughes wrote the screenplay in a week and secured a $6-million budget to shoot the film in Chicago. Ferris encourages his depressed school friend Cameron Frye (Alan Ruck) to help him break girlfriend Sloane Peterson (Mia Sara) out of school so they can enjoy touring the city in Frye's father's immaculate 1961 Ferrari California Spyder, which Bueller somehow manages to convince Cameron to lend him. Bueller's jealous and angry sister Jeanie (Jennifer Grey) and the school's psychotic dean, Edward Rooney (Jeffrey Jones), see through the deception and desperately try to catch Bueller so that he'll be expelled.

Only around 50 Ferrari 250GT's with the short wheelbase were built so none could be bought or damaged during filming. (In 2008 DJ Chris Evans bought James Coburn's black 1961 SWB 250GT for a record price of £5.5 million.) Indeed the wide shots in the film were of a fibreglass-bodied replica based on an MG, although plenty of insert shots used a real 250GT.

The original car was exhibited at the 1960 Geneva Motorshow. It had an updated chassis over its predecessor, the 250 Berlinetta, disc brakes all round and a 276bhp 3-litre V12 engine. John Hughes had read about a company in California (Modena Design and Development) that produced replicas of the 250. He was impressed with their version so he commissioned vehicle restoration specialist Mark Goyette to produce three kit cars.

The first was leased to Paramount and

was the one that jumped over the camera. When the production company returned it to Goyette after filming it had sustained minor damage so he restored it and sold it. It last turned up in 2000 but hasn't been seen since.

The second Goyette car was sold to Paramount as a stunt car but the kit wasn't usable except when it needed to be driven out of the window at the Cameron residence. (Ferris had left the car with an attendant in a car park but the attendant had then driven round the city for hours. When Cameron saw the milometer had changed and it became clear that the car had been driven all day, he realised his father would explode. The pair decide to rectify the problem by jacking up the car and putting it into reverse to wind back the clock, which doesn't work of course. In a fit of rage, Cameron then kicks the front of the car, unbalancing it from the jack. With the wheels still spinning in reverse, it launches itself out of the garage into a ravine behind the house.) This replica was then rebuilt and shipped to the Planet Hollywood restaurant in Minneapolis. It ended up in Planet Hollywood, Cancun, before the latter outlet closed. The last only made it as far as a shell, although it was rumoured to have been finished eventually.

Ferris Bueller's Day Off remains one of the iconic films of the 1980s.

Cheech and Chong's Van

Opposite:
Cheech and
Chong's van was
made entirely
from hardened
marijuana resin

Richard 'Cheech' Marin and Tommy Chong met in Vancouver in the late 1960s. The pair shared a mutual love of quirky comedy and soon developed an award-winning stand-up routine that was based on the hippie- and soft-drug counterculture of the era and also included songs penned by the duo.

Then, in 1978, they decided to make a feature film. Despite having a tiny budget, the result was the cult classic *Up In Smoke*, a story about two cannabis enthusiasts who meet when Anthony Stoner (Chong) breaks down by the side of the road and accepts a lift from Pedro de Pacas (Cheech Marin). The pair find themselves in all manner of scrapes and eventually end up driving a van made entirely of hardened marijuana resin from Mexico to Los Angeles while the inept cops try to stop them.

Despite the budget, somewhat erratic script and production values, and the controversial content, the film grossed $44 million and became the 15th most successful movie of 1978. The star, of course, was the van, which incapacitated just about every human and animal (particularly the sniffer dog) that came near it. Indeed when it catches fire and the smoke is channelled into the building where a battle-of-the-bands contest is being held, everyone in the audience and the ever-present cops get completely wasted. Follow-up movies were less successful.

The 1971 Lincoln Continental Mark III from The Car

The Car was a low-budget horror film about a driverless car that goes on the rampage through the fictional town of Santa Ynez in Utah. As the body count rises, Captain Wade Parent (James Brolin) is assigned to hunt the evil car down and destroy hit, his personal mission becoming a vendetta when the vehicle crashes through his girlfriend's house, killing her while they were on the phone. The police eventually decide to lure the demonic car into the canyons outside the town so they can bury it in a controlled explosion. Although the plan appears to work, the car is once again seen stalking potential victims as the credits roll.

Legendary Hollywood carman George Barris was given the job of customising the 1971 Lincoln Continental. He was given four cars, of which three were used for stunt work and the fourth was used for close-ups. The rigours of stunt driving were too much for the designated cars and they were all destroyed during filming. The fourth car is now in a private collection. The film was a commercial failure and was panned by viewers for the quality of the script and acting, although it has since been listed as one of the top 100 most enjoyable bad movies.

Eleanor from Gone in 60 Seconds

The 1974 version of the film *Gone in 60 Seconds* starred Toby Halicki as insurance investigator Maindrian Pace. He ran a respectable chop shop in Long Beach but moonlighted as the leader of a gang of car thieves who stole insured vehicles to order. Pace was contacted by a drugs baron and asked to steal 48 cars in return for $400,000. The cars had to be delivered to the Long Beach docks within five days, however. Pace accepted the deal even though several of the vehicles were rare or unusual (limousines or trucks, for example).

Each vehicle was given a female codename and most of the thefts went according to plan, but one car in particular proved troublesome: a yellow 1973 Ford Mustang nicknamed Eleanor (the actual car was a 1971 Sportsroof variant that was modified to look like the 1973 model).

The team failed to steal the first two they found but then manage to procure one relatively easily. Just before they delivered it to the docks, however, Eleanor was found to be uninsured so Pace had to return it. He then found a fourth match and promptly stole it, thereby setting up the film's climatic car chase, during which 93 other cars were destroyed. As Eleanor was so badly damaged during the chase, Pace had to swap it for a fifth car at a petrol station before finally heading for the docks.

Halicki wrote, directed, produced and starred in the low-budget caper, and he also did most of his own stunts, some of which went wrong. When his car span out of control on the freeway and struck a streetlight he was badly hurt, and the Eleanor jump at the film's climax saw him compact 10 vertebrae. Indeed there was

no official script and his friends and family even played parts. Most of the bystanders were real people unaware that they were in a film. Despite this leading to huge problems for the editing team, the result was a creditable B-Movie. For a film with a budget of just $150,000 it was a surprise hit and took $40 million at the box office. Despite the incidences of stunts going wrong, the stunt car itself survives to this day.

In 1989 Halicki began shooting a sequel but only a few weeks in a stunt went wrong and he was killed by a sheared telephone pole. His widow, Denice, vowed to complete the project and she eventually helped produce the Nicholas Cage remake in 2000. This time the Eleanor car was a 1967 Shelby Ford Mustang Fastback GT500. One of the cars used during filming sold at auction in 2013 for $1 million. The film itself took nearly $250 million on a budget of $90 million but, when all overheads and expenses were factored in, it apparently lost nearly $100 million.

Above: *The 1967 Shelby Ford Mustang GT500 from the 2000 remake*

The 1967 Pontiac GTO from xXx

XXx was an action/adventure film starring Vin Diesel as Xander Cage, a thrill-seeking athlete who is recruited to the National Security Agency by Augustus Gibbons (Samuel L. Jackson) to infiltrate a Russian terrorist cell. Anarchy 99 supposedly has a chemical weapon missing since the break-up of the Soviet Union but, as the cell has always rooted out government agents by their predictable behaviour, Gibbons decides to use Cage as a mole as he can handle himself in difficult situations and doesn't have any formal intelligence training.

Of course no secret agent would be sent abroad without some form of transportation, and Cage is supplied with a gadget- and weapon-laden purple 1967 Pontiac GTO. Converting the everyday road-going version into the superspy's

personal war machine fell to Eddie Paul's E.P. Industries, which has been customising, restoring, wrecking and rebuilding cars such as Sylvester Stallone's brutal Mercury Monterey Coupe from Cobra and dozens of high-performance muscle cars for *The Fast and the Furious*.

As the 1967 Pontiac GTO was reasonably rare, Paul placed an ad and made some calls asking for people with clean running examples to bring them to the workshop and they would be paid above the current value. Around seven cars were chosen, with up to $20,000 then being spent on modifying each to the industry standard for stunt work, close-ups and wide shots prior to filming in Prague in the Czech Republic.

The cars were then put through their paces during a gruelling shooting schedule that saw them get through 200

sets of tyres. After filming, most were in such a state that they were left in Prague. Legendary restorer George Barris added more gadgets to three that survived so they could be used on promotional tours, while another ended up on eBay. Rainmakers movie props then sold one at auction for $38,300.

Above: *Xander Cage's Pontiac GTO from xXx*

The 1932 Ford Coupe from American Graffiti

American Graffiti is an American film from renowned writer and director George Lucas. Set against the rock-and-roll counterculture of California in the early '60s, it follows the lives of a group of teenagers cruising the strip on their last night before heading off to college.

Lucas drew inspiration from his own adolescent life when he came up with the characters (indeed many seem to be younger versions of the director throughout his youth). Although he then worked with several writers developing the script, he felt they all wanted to add overtly sexual references or scenes that didn't reflect the coming-of-age feel he had in mind for the film.

Lucas also found it difficult to get backing for the project. Despite spending two years working on the script and pitching the idea to MGM, Paramount,

20th Century Fox and Columbia, he was rejected by all of them. American International Pictures did show some interest but they wanted to rewrite the script to include the sex and violence that Lucas had spent years trying to avoid. Universal Pictures eventually came to the rescue but they only provided a budget of $600,000 because they felt Lucas, who wanted complete control over the shooting schedule and the script, was relatively inexperienced. When Francis Ford Coppola signed on to produce the movie, Universal provided an extra $175,000. The overall box office and home-video take was well over $150 million so *American Graffiti* became one of the most profitable films of all time. It also received universal praise for the writing and directing and was nominated for the Academy Award for Best Picture (it lost

Above: *The 1932 Ford Coupe*

to *The Sting*). It made George Lucas a millionaire overnight and allowed him the freedom to develop his space opera project that eventually became *Star Wars*.

One of the abiding memories from a film that the US Library of Congress deemed culturally, historically or aesthetically significant in 1995 was the yellow 1932 Ford Coupe. Henry Travers oversaw the coupe's transformation into a hot rod, which was completed at Bob Hamilton's workshop in Ignacio. The car had motorbike fenders, aluminium headlight stanchions, chrome plating, a new grill and modified shell. Then an intake manifold and four Rochester twin-barrel carburettors were added to the 1966 Chevrolet 327 V8, along with an upgraded exhaust system and bespoke interior. Despite having an asking price of only around $2,000, the vehicle remained unsold after shooting had wrapped. It is now in the hands of San Francisco collector Rick Figari.

Scooby-Doo's Mystery Machine

Scooby-Doo is an American cartoon series that first aired in 1969 and is still running today. It was another animation from the Hanna-Barbera production team who had also brought *Tom and Jerry*, *Droopy* and *The Flintstones* to the small screen. The premise behind *Scooby-Doo* was that four teenagers – Fred Jones, Daphne Blake, Velma Dinkley and Norville 'Shaggy' Rogers – would drive around the country in their Mystery Machine investigating supposedly supernatural happenings with their talkative but cowardly Great Dane, Scooby-Doo.

Despite pitching several ideas to executives in the mid-1960s, William Hanna and Joseph Barbera couldn't find any takers for the show until they'd developed the characters further and the dog's name had been changed from Too Much to Scooby-Doo. CBS broadcast the show's original run until 1976, although ABC then took it on until 1986. Various other networks have since aired subsequent series, some of which featured Scooby's small but feisty nephew Scrappy-Doo.

The Mystery Machine was the team's psychedelic van, which often helped them get out of scrapes but usually drove them into yet another scary situation. Several real versions of the Mystery Machine have been built, with the most common being based on a 1963 Ford Econoline Custom van or a 1972 Bedford CF.

Above: *One of the many live-action incarnations of Scooby-Doo's Mystery Machine*

The Volkswagen Beetle from The Love Bug

Herbie is a pearl white 1963 Volkswagen Beetle that appeared in several Disney films, beginning with *The Love Bug* (1969), which was based on the 1961 book *Car, Boy, Girl* by Gordon Buford. The car is bought from the stuffy Peter Thorndyke (David Tomlinson) by a local socialite for her maid, but Mrs Van Luit returns it immediately due to reliability problems. It is then sold to racing driver Jim Douglas (Dean Jones), the man who stood up for the car while it was berated by Thorndyke. Jim's roommate Tennessee Steinmetz (Buddy Hackett) christens the car Herbie after his uncle.

Jim can't help feeling duped when the car begins to spin out of control as if it has a mind of its own. Tennessee then convinces him that some inanimate objects have souls and that this incredible car must be one of them. As it has a searing top speed for such an underpowered vehicle, and Jim has no more cars in his garage, the pair enter the car in a series of races.

Their successes bring them to the attention of Thorndyke, himself a dab hand behind the wheel. Thorndyke challenges Jim to a number of races but Herbie condemns him to humiliating defeats. Thorndyke exacts revenge by pouring alcoholic Irish cream into the car's petrol tank and racing to victory the following day with Herbie completely out of sorts. Jim therefore decides to sell the Beetle in exchange for a Lamborghini so he can compete in the big El Dorado road race. Herbie is less than pleased and destroys the Lamborghini before rampaging around San Francisco and eventually trying to drive off the Golden Gate Bridge. Jim finally convinces Herbie that he needs

Above: *The Love Bug, Herbie*

him for the race and, despite Thorndyke's increasingly dirty tricks, the pair eventually take victory.

Several cars 'auditioned' for the role but the cast and crew all favoured the Beetle. Its racing number (53) was chosen by producer Bill Walsh because that was LA Dodgers' baseball player Don Drysdale's shirt number. He also insisted on the car's colour scheme and devised many of the films visual gags. Herbie was the first of only two cars ever to be credited in a film, the second being Eleanor, the Ford Mustang from the original *Gone in 60 Seconds* movie. Very few of the original cars used in the film are known to exist. Four cinematic sequels also featured the car as the star, while a number of TV movies have resurrected the character in the intervening years.

The Munster Koach from The Munsters

The Munsters was an American television sitcom chronicling the lives of a family of monsters. It was created by Allan Burns and Chris Hayward, developed by Norm Liebmann and Ed Haas, and released by CBS to counter the threat from ABC's *The Addams Family*, which was a series about a family of gothic humans with supernatural powers. Although it only lasted two seasons and 70 episodes between 1964 and 1966 (the arrival of *Batman*, which was filmed in colour, severely impacted the ratings), it became a cult classic that has stood the test of time and been broadcast around the world ever since.

While the characters were broadly similar to those on *The Addams Family*, the Munsters were a working-class and outgoing family. As Universal produced the show, they could draw on the classic horror characters that were created by the studio in the 1920s and '30s. Herman, for example, was essentially Frankenstein. The family lived in a crumbling Victorian mansion in the fictional suburb of Los Angeles known as Mockingbird Heights.

The family car, the Munster Koach, became a star in its own right. The producers wanted something that would be instantly recognisable so they contacted George Barris at Barris Kustoms and he, Tex Smith and Dick Dean came up with a hot rod-type vehicle based on a 1926 Ford Model T. It was built on an elongated chassis with a custom hearse body at a cost of $20,000.

Only one Koach was built for the entire series. It was 18 feet long (which required three Ford chassis), had brass radiators and bumpers, ten air horns, lantern lights, blood-red interior, hand-formed roll-

steel scrollworks and gloss black paint. Power came from a 289-cubic-inch (4.7-litre) Ford V8 that would normally have gone into an AC Cobra. It had high-compression pistons, 10 chrome-plated carburettors, racing headers and a three-speed manual transmission.

An unauthorised replica was built and then bought by members of Barris's team, although it was later sold to Jay Ohrberg. Barris auctioned the original in 1982 but he then asked Dick Dean to build him another. This was restored in 2011 with a number of optional extras.

A second car designed by Tom Daniel and built by Richard Korkes at Barris Kustoms was based on a real coffin. Herman had lost the Koach in a drag race so a new vehicle was needed to win it back. The 1966 DRAG-U-LA had a similar 289-cubic-inch (4.7-litre) Ford V8, which produced 350bhp and had a four-speed manual transmission. It was fitted with Firestone racing slicks and sported a gothic motif. This car was sold at auction in 1985 and ended up hanging from the ceiling of Planet Hollywood in Atlantic City. When the restaurant closed, the car was restored by the Volo Auto Museum in Illinois.

The Monkeemobile from The Monkees

The idea of forming a band and developing a television show, both of which would eventually lead to *The Monkees*, was inspired by the success of The Beatles' film *A Hard Day's Night*. Producers and aspiring filmmakers Bob Rafelson and Bert Schneider pitched an idea to NBC about a fictional rock and roll band, and a draft script was then penned by Paul Mazursky and Larry Tucker.

In much the same way as *Pop Idol* and *X-Factor*, the producers then placed adverts in local trade publications for singers who wanted to appear in a new TV show. Hundreds of hopefuls were whittled down to 14, after which a final four were selected: Micky Dolenz had appeared on screen before and was already auditioning for roles; Englishman Davy Jones had some recording and performing experience; Michael Nesmith had recorded on the Columbia

Pictures (Colpix) record label; and the multi-talented Peter Tork was recommended by Stephen Stills.

The series drew heavily on European influences, particularly The Beatles, but it also pioneered the use of quick cuts, breaking the fourth wall (speaking directly to the audience) and introducing a song, almost as a precursor to today's music videos. Each of the four stars was given a new personality (although it was based on their real selves) and taught to improvise comedic dialogue.

The pilot wasn't well received but it was reshot within two days and proved much more successful. The theme tune then became a hit and the series was up and running. The Monkees' pad, a two-storey beach house in Malibu, was quickly established so all the group needed now was a car.

The outrageous Monkeemobile was

designed and built by Dean Jeffries. It was a modified 389-cubic-inch (6.4-litre) 4-barrel 1966 Pontiac GTO with a split windscreen, completely redesigned panels and bumpers, bucket seats and a parachute. Extra weight was stowed in the rear so that the overpowered brute could pull wheelies.

Two cars were built, of which one was used by the TV show while the other was taken on promotional tours. Jeffries was under contract with the Model Products Corporation so he made sure the company got the rights to built replica kits, of which they eventually sold seven million units.

The TV car was offered to Jeffries after filming but, as he could build a new one cheaper, he declined. It was left behind in Australia after a tour in 1968 and then somehow found its way to Puerto Rico where it was used as a hotel's courtesy car. When the hotel went bust in 1992, the car was sold at auction and partially restored. It is now part of a private collection.

As Jeffries also refused to buy the touring show car, it went to George Barris (he of the Munster Koach fame). Barris exhibited the car at all kinds of events before having it completely restored in 2006. Two years later the incredible car was sold at auction to a private collector for $360,000. The team behind the original cars also built the odd copy for promotional reasons, and many unauthorised replicas are also in circulation. An authorised tribute car was then built for the Monkees' 45th Anniversary Tour in 2011. This was the last reunion for all the band members as Davy Jones died from a heart attack in 2012.

Lady Penelope's Rolls-Royce from Thunderbirds

Thunderbirds was a British science-fiction adventure series from the creative team of Gerry and Sylvia Anderson. Although it only lasted for 32 episodes between 1964 and 1966, the intricate puppetry, incredible scale models and stunning special effects (from the team that developed James Bond's amphibious Lotus Esprit) meant that it became more popular than the 'supermarionation' shows that preceded it, notably *Supercar* and *Stingray*.

The story followed the exploits of Jeff Tracy's secretive International Rescue outfit, which used advanced Thunderbird machines (piloted by his five sons) to rescue those in danger and thwart the dastardly plots of a criminal entity known as the Hood. Tracy ran his day-to-day operation from a luxurious villa on an uncharted island in the South Pacific.

The Thunderbird fleet, meanwhile, was designed by scientist Brains and could be launched from a subsurface base.

Thunderbird 1 was a hypersonic rocket plane flown by Scott; Thunderbird 2 was a supersonic heavy-lift transport vehicle under Virgil's command; Thunderbird 3 was a single-stage spacecraft controlled by Alan; Thunderbird 4 was a submarine piloted by Gordon; and Thunderbird 5 was a space station in geostationary orbit. Their missions were primarily humanitarian but, when criminal investigations were launched, the organisation relied on collecting information from a network of intelligence agents, two of whom happened to be English aristocrat Lady Penelope Creighton-Ward and her butler/chauffeur Aloysius 'Nosey' Parker. Lady Penelope's car was a

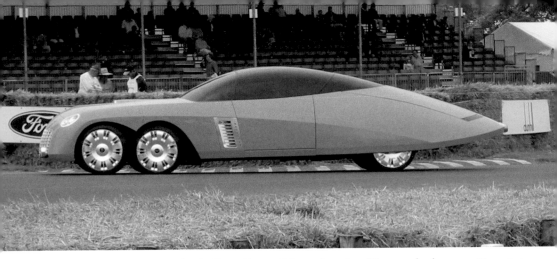

magnificent amphibious pink Rolls-Royce.

The six-wheeled car had a centrally mounted driving position, bullet-proof passenger compartment, front and rear machineguns, twin lasers, harpoon launchers, grappling hooks, smoke screen, oil slick, extendable tyre studs, hydrofoil outriggers and amphibious conversion. With a Rolls-Royce gas turbine engine it was apparently capable of 200mph on land and, thanks to propulsion from a vortex aquajet, 50 knots in water.

A full-size working replica based on the chassis of a Bedford Duple Vega was built in 1966 to carry the Andersons to the premiere of *Thunderbirds Are Go*. It had a six-cylinder petrol engine,

Powerglide gearbox, Land Rover wheels, Perspex sides, custom-built radiator grille and an imitation machinegun. The car broke down on its way to the premiere and Rolls-Royce then spent years trying to buy it so that it could be destroyed. It eventually underwent a full restoration and was sold in 2013 to the Dezer Car Museum in Florida when the Cars of the Stars Museum in Cumbria closed down.

A different version was built for the big-budget live-action adaptation in 2004. It was a heavily modified Ford Thunderbird (what else!) that was both functional and roadworthy. It was tested by James May from *Top Gear* and now resides in the Heritage Motor Centre in Warwickshire.

Above: *Lady Penelope always travels in style*

The Panthermobile from The Pink Panther

The Pink Panther was a series of cartoon shorts mixed with live action that aired on NBC and ABC in the United States from 1969 until 1980. Produced by David DePatie of Warner Brothers Cartoons fame, and animator and cartoonist Friz Freleng who either created or developed *Bugs Bunny*, *Porky Pie* and *Yosemite Sam* (amongst many others), the characters of the Pink Panther and inept French inspector had first appeared during the opening credits to the eponymous 1963 film starring Peter Sellers as Inspector Jacques Clouseau. While Henry Mancini's popular jazzy theme tune played, the inspector would desperately try to capture the elusive panther in much the same way as Wile E. Coyote hunted the Roadrunner.

Such was the success of the opening sequence with studio executives that they commissioned DePatie-Freleng Enterprises to develop the idea into a series of cartoon shorts, the first of which appeared in 1964 and promptly won the Academy Award for Best Animated Short Film. This is the only time that a studio's first release has won an Oscar. By 1969 the shorts were being broadcast on NBC and the live action sequences had introduced a bizarre pink car.

The one-of-a-kind vehicle was designed and built by Bob Reisner, Dan Woods, Joe Bailon, Bill Hines and Bill Honda of California Show Cars for around $100,000. It was based on the chassis of an Oldsmobile Tornado that allowed a central driving position in front of a (*Playboy*-inspired) pleasure capsule. It was then sold to Jay Ohrberg (the man behind the Batmobile, KITT and Marty

McFly's time-travelling DoLorean from *Back to the Future*). In 2007 Ohrberg sold the car at auction for £88,000 but its unusual shape and lack of safety features meant it wasn't roadworthy. It was sold again in 2011 to a private collector.

Mach 5 Speed Racer

Speed Racer, which was also known as *Mach GoGoGo*, was a Japanese animated series based around car racing in the 1960s. It was originally released as a comic by Sun Wide but was then adapted for the screen by Tatsunoko Productions. Fuji TV then broadcast 52 episodes between 1967 and 1968, but it took a while before the series was taken up by other broadcasters around the world.

The original hero was Go Mifune who was famous for his car, the Mach 5, and his passion for motorsport. The cartoon car was probably based on an early (1958) Scaglietti-designed Ferrari 250 Testa Rossa, although it was also influenced by the Ford GT40, which was trouncing the opposition at Le Mans at the time. There are also traces of the Chaparral 2C and Alfa Romeo 33.2, the latter of which was a concept car designed by Pininfarina.

The car had inbuilt jacks so it could be repaired easily, special tyres that could adapt to any terrain, a 5,000bhp engine delivering power evenly to all four wheels, rotary saws for slicing through obstacles, crash-proof cockpit, night-vision systems, submarine conversion and a homing device to return the car to Speed's house.

In 2006 producer Joel Silver rescued a project based on the animation that had been languishing in development hell since 1992. He approached the famous Wachowski directing duo and the pair also agreed to write a new script for a live-action feature film. As the story was based in Berlin, the movie became a German/American production with a budget of $120 million.

Speed Racer (Emile Hersch) always

looked up to his older brother but, when Rex (Scott Porter) was killed during a rally, Speed decided to continue racing in his sibling's memory. Rex's car was the Mach 5, which Speed brought out of retirement when his Mach 6 was destroyed. Despite its huge budget and A-list cast, the film was a commercial failure, although rumours still circulate that a sequel could be in the offing.

Above: *The live-action version of the Mach 5 Speed Racer*

Roary the Racing Car

Opposite: *Roary the racing car with Big Chris*

Roary the Racing Car is a British animated adventure set at the fictional Silver Hatch track (Silver Hatch obviously being a portmanteau of Silverstone and Brands Hatch, the UK's two most famous circuits). The series focuses on Roary's exploits, along with those of his friends and rivals like Maxi, Cici and Tin Top, as well as the human characters.

The production team uses a mix of CGI technology and stop-motion animation to bring the characters to life. Each episode opens with an introduction from arguably Britain's most famous driver, Sir Stirling Moss, while IndyCar and NASCAR champion Sam Hornish Junior introduces the US version. So far the series has run for four seasons and 104 episodes but, such is its popularity, it looks set to run for some time yet. It has also been taken up by international broadcasters and is shown in territories worldwide.

The star of the show is Roary (voiced by Maria Darling), an enthusiastic single-seat racing car who is mechanic Big Chris's pride and joy (Chris is voiced by comedian Peter Kay). He wears a white baseball cap with a number '1' on a red star in its centre. The character is young and inexperienced but he soon learns the intricacies of racing from Maxi (Marc Silk), an old Formula 1 car, and Cici (Maria Darling), a flirtatious stunt car who repeatedly challenges Roary to catch or race her. As with most shows of this kind, merchandising is a key revenue stream and toys from the series are universally popular.

The Cars from Hot Wheels Battle Force 5

Hot Wheels Battle Force 5 is a 3D CGI TV series created for the Cartoon Network by American toy makers Mattel, Canadian entertainment company Nelvana, and Nerd Corps Entertainment, a Canadian computer animation studio in Vancouver.

The premise has racing driver Vert Wheeler joining forces with a sentient life-form called Sage. Together they assemble a team of racing cars to compete against Sark (a robot) and his team of Vandals. Both sides upgrade their cars with specialised chips, which gives them access to weapons and a host of other gadgets they will need as they fight for control of battle zones throughout the universe.

Battle Force 5 is based at Wheeler's circuit in the town of Handler's Corners. Their headquarters are in his subterranean garage known as The Hub. Portals to different dimensions allow the team to compete against enemies for control of a number of keys. Earth's Key must be protected from the Vandals to prevent Sark taking over the planet.

The Homer from The Simpsons

The Simpsons is an adult-oriented American animation whereby the dialogue appeals to a more mature audience and the often slapstick action is more suitable for children who don't get the older humour. It follows the exploits of a splendidly dysfunctional family and, since first airing as a series of shorts on the *Tracey Ullman Show* in 1987 and then as its own series in 1989, it has gone on to win countless awards (28 Emmys for starters) for its 550 episodes (and counting).

Homer (voiced by Dan Castellaneta) is the buffoon at the head of the family, while the long-suffering Marge (Julie Kavner) is his wife. Their son Bart (Nancy Cartwright) is a mischievous but loveable rogue who is always in trouble at home and school, while his younger sister Lisa (Yeardley Smith) is the polar opposite:

bright, straight-laced and a keen activist on humanitarian issues. The youngest sister, Maggie, communicates by sucking on a dummy.

Homer is a safety inspector at a nuclear powerplant, a position totally unsuited to the clumsy and careless person that he is. In one of his many hiatuses from work, he is offered a job by his half-brother Herb designing cars for Powell Motors. Homer decides to build a car for the average American, which of course means he has no concept of the brief or the cost of the monstrosity that he designs.

The Homer has two passenger bubble compartments, with the rearmost usually used for bickering children (it also has optional restraints). The engine note has been worked on fastidiously so buyers believe the world is coming to an end. Because Homer could never find the

Above: *The Homer*

horn in time, he built this concept with three, all of which played *La Cucarachara*. The car also has enormous cup holders, shag carpets, giant tailfins and various ornaments about its bodywork. The end result was so expensive that Powell Motors went bust and the workshop was sold to Komatsu Motors instead.

Despite criticisms that the show is getting a little tired and formulaic after 25 years, and that it now relies on outlandish plots rather than character-driven stories, it still retains a global popularity that other shows find impossible to match. It is no exaggeration to say that the family are national treasures in almost every territory.

Postman Pat's Van

Postman Pat is a stop-motion animation series about Pat Clifton, a postman in the village of Greendale. It was created by author John Cunliffe (who based Greendale on settlements in the Longsleddale Valley near Kendal in Cumbria) and animator Ivor Wood (*The Magic Roundabout*, *Paddington Bear*) and first aired on UK television in 1981.

Pat and his black-and-white cat Jess deliver the post in the valley in Pat's familiar red van. Although his round should be routine, Pat always becomes distracted by villagers who invariably need help. He's a kind-hearted soul so he always lends a hand.

Pat's first van (registration PAT1) was a small box van based on the BMC/Leyland Sherpa. It became his transport for the first seven episodes of series one. The Royal Mail eventually allowed the program makers to use their gold crest on the van because the character promoted the company and was watched by millions.

By 1991 Pat had taken the wheel of a fleet service postbus (PAT2), which could carry passengers and freight. It was then painted yellow and transformed into the local school bus. In the most recent series, Pat has been promoted to the head of the Special Delivery Service, so his SDS van is much larger. During his travels in the valley, Pat also uses an SDS helicopter, a minivan and motorbike (with a sidecar for Jess), a quad-bike and a post car for urgent deliveries.

With broadcasters around the world showing the series, it was decided that a feature-length version should be released. In early 2014 a computer-animated 3D movie was shown in cinemas across the

Above: *Postman Pat with his van and Jess*

UK. It was produced by Lionsgate Films and Icon Productions, and animated by RGH Pictures. Stephen Mangan voiced Pat, while David Tennant, Rupert Grint and Jim Broadbent also had roles.

Longleat House has since built an outdoor scale reproduction of the village. The theme tune became a hit when Wogan played it every morning on BBC Radio 2's breakfast show in the early 1980s.

Fred Flintstone's Car

The Flintstones was another popular cartoon from the creative team of William Hanna and Joseph Barbera. It ran for six years and 167 episodes between 1960 and 1966. In 2013 it came second to *The Simpsons* in a *TV Guide* poll to find the greatest animated series of all time. As Joseph Barbera explained, however, finding a network to take the show in the first place wasn't straightforward.

"I pitched it for eight straight weeks and nobody bought it. So, after sitting in New York feeling worn from pitching up to five times a day, I finally pitched it to ABC, which was a young and daring network willing to try new things. They bought the show in 15 minutes. Thank goodness, because this was the last day I was prepared to pitch and if they hadn't bought it I would have taken everything down, put it in the archives and never pitched it again. Sometimes I wake up in a cold sweat thinking how close we came to disaster."

The cartoon was set in the stone-age town of Bedrock, although dinosaurs and other prehistoric creatures that should have been extinct happily co-existed with cavemen who have developed precursors to many modern conveniences (record players, cars, cameras, vacuum cleaners etc). These gadgets were invariably powered by the animals, however, such as the mammoths providing the showers, brontosauruses manning the lifts, and woodpeckers using their beaks as styluses on the gramophones. In the case of Fred Flintstone's car, power came from the family themselves, their feet dangling through the floor so they could run along the road.

Fred was a clumsy crane operator at the local quarry. His quick temper belied a good nature and a clear love for his family, however. Wife Wilma always kept a level head and provided the counterpoint to Fred's belligerence. Their neighbours were Barney and Betty Rubble, with whom the Flintstones shared many adventures and mini feuds.

The show spawned many spinoffs like *The Pebbles and Bamm-Bamm Show*

(named after the Flintsones' and the Rubbles' children respectively), as well as live-action feature films in 1994 (starring John Goodman as Fred and Rick Moranis as Barney) and a less successful prequel in 2000. For all its many incarnations, Fred's car with its stone body, wooden wheels, animal skin roof and unique method of human propulsion remains as popular today as when it first appeared more than half a century ago.

Above: *Fred Flintstone with his Stone Age car*

The Cars from Wacky Races

*W*acky Races was an American cartoon from William Hanna and Joseph Barbera that aired on CBS between 1968 and 1969. The original idea had been to have a live-action quiz show based on the race and its outcome but this concept was eventually shelved so only the animated series remained.

The evil Dick Dastardly (voiced by Paul Winchell) and his anthropomorphic dog henchman Muttley (Don Messick) were the villains of the series. Their car, the Mean Machine, was a purple rocket-powered beast so they were by far the fastest of all the racers. Despite roaring into a big lead, Dastardly would then stop to lay traps for the chasing pack. However, the traps invariably backfired and always cost him victory. As he was unable not to cheat, Dastardly never finished a race in the top three and he

only finished five of 17 races overall. The characters were so successful that Dastardly and Muttley eventually earned their own TV show.

Penelope Pitstop (Janet Waldo) was the only female amongst the racers. Her car, the Compact Pussycat, was a smart pink convertible that she tended to use as a mobile beauty parlour rather than a racing car. When it broke down, which was often, the other racers would either stop to help or would refuse to overtake her until her mechanical issues were solved. Such was the popularity of the character that she too ended up with her own series – *The Perils of Penelope Pitstop* – which also featured her rivals in the Wacky Races, the Ant Hill Mob.

The Ant Hill Mob's vehicle of choice was the Bulletproof Bomb, a 1920s-style limousine that had room for all seven

Wacky Races™

Above: *Dastardly and Muttley in their Mean Machine from Wacky Races*

gangsters on the front seat. To increase power, the tiny team would stick their feet through the floor and run in much the same way as the car in *The Flintstones*. When in trouble, the Ant Hill Mob would occasionally draw their Tommy guns and fire on the other competitors. In the spinoff starring Penelope Pitstop, they were always riding to her rescue in a new car: Chugga-Boom.

Lightning McQueen from Cars

Cars is a Pixar CGI adventure/comedy set in a world populated by anthropomorphic vehicles, in which racing car Lightning McQueen (voiced by Owen Wilson) is the hero. Lightning McQueen is desperate to win the last race of the season at the Los Angeles International Speedway so that he can earn sponsorship money and compete for the prestigious Dinoco team. He is praised for his sportsmanship when pushing a rival across the line, and also helps put the town of Radiator Springs back on the map. The film was a huge commercial success, returning nearly $500 million on a budget of $120 million, and the merchandising apparently topped $10 billion. *Cars 2*, which was released in 2011, was an even bigger success at the box office.

The car itself was named after animator Glenn McQueen who died of cancer in 2002. It was based on the shape of a NASCAR but also borrowed design features from a Dodge Viper and a Mazda Miata, and its custom livery resembled the paint job Corvette gave the C1. The Pixar team then had to give the car character so they drew on cocky but likeable figures from the world of sport and entertainment, Muhammad Ali and Kid Rock in particular. For the car's movement, the animators also looked at the fluidity and grace of sports stars like Michael Jordan.

Such was the popularity of the character that Pixar wrote a video game that acted as a continuation of the movie. The sequel introduced McQueen to another legion of fans, and in March 2014 Pixar announced that *Cars 3* was already in pre-production.

Chitty Chitty Bang Bang

Chitty Chitty Bang Bang is a 1968 film based on Bond author Ian Fleming's novel about a magical car. Roald Dahl and Ken Hughes penned the screenplay, while the Sherman Brothers wrote the music and Cubby Broccoli produced. The film starred Dick van Dyke as madcap inventor Caractacus Potts and Sally Ann Bowles as Truly Scrumptious.

A local garage owner has salvaged the remains of a car that had won several races on the continent but which had then crashed. A junkman expresses interest in the car so he can melt it down for scrap metal but Potts's two children, Jeremy and Jemima, adore the wreck and beg their father to rescue it. Potts doesn't have the money but he eventually cobbles together enough to save the car, which he then rebuilds and christens Chitty Chitty Bang Bang on account of the noises it makes.

Word of the incredible car spreads until it reaches the evil Baron Bomburst of Vulgaria. The baron dispatches spies to steal it but they kidnap Grandpa Potts and escape in an airship instead. The rest of the Potts family and Truly give chase in Chitty Chitty Bang Bang, which takes to the air having driven off a cliff. The family must then rescue Grandpa and evade the baron and his child-catcher.

The inspiration for the car came from the aero-engined pre-war racers built by Count Louis Zborowski in the 1920s. Six versions of the magical car were built for the film, although only one was road-legal. It was designed by Ken Adam (another Bond connection) and cartoonist Frederick Rowland Emett, and then built by Alan Mann Racing in

Above: A road-legal replica of the magical Chitty Chitty Bang Bang

1967. It had a 3-litre Ford V6 engine, automatic transmission and was given a proper UK registration number.

This road-going version was in the private collection of Stratford's Pierre Picton from 1971 until 2011, whereupon it fetched $805,000 at auction in Los Angeles. Two more cars have been exhibited at museums across the UK, while a smaller model was in the Cars of the Stars Museum in Keswick, Cumbria, until the museum closed in 2011. Yet another privately owned incarnation, that of Anthony Bamford, is on show at the National Motor Museum in Hampshire. Another of the cars that was actually used on screen was on display in a restaurant in Chicago in 2007 before being sold at auction for $505,000 to a collector in Florida. A copy built for the stage production at the London Palladium in 2002 broke the world record for the most expensive prop ever made (£750,000).

The Flying Car from The Jetsons

The Jetsons was an American animation from the Hanna-Barbera stable that ran for 75 episodes between 1962-3 and 1985-7. Although penned by the same team as *The Flintstones*, *The Jetsons* was the polar opposite in that the series was set in Orbit City in 2062. In this futuristic utopia, all manner of advanced contraptions existed, from robots to aliens and sentient holograms.

George Jetson was the head of the family. He was a kind and considerate family man who always seemed to make the wrong decision. Wife Jane was the homemaker who was also obsessed with the latest gadgets. Daughter Judy was a stereotypical teenager at Orbit High School, while her younger bother, Elroy, was a highly intelligent science whiz. The family robot, Rosie, was outdated but they refused to trader her for a more recent model because she did all the housework and looked after the kids.

The writers did a remarkable job of predicting the future in that they included two-way videophones, flat-screen TVs, robotic vacuum cleaners and handheld tablet devices that broadcast the news, but the flying car they foresaw hasn't yet arrived. Granted, George's bubble-top high-octane-pellet- and radium-powered car could be folded down into a briefcase so it was probably made of a multistate carbon-based shape-shifting polymer that we don't have yet, but flying cars may be closer than we think. The Moller Skycar and Terrafugia TF-X could be here by 2025…

The pictures in this book were provided courtesy of the following:

WIKICOMMONS
commons.wikimedia.org

Design & Artwork by Scott Giarnese

Published by Demand Media Limited

Publishers: Jason Fenwick & Jules Gammond

Written by Liam McCann